MADE 4 MORE

21 DAYS OF EXPERIENCING GOD'S LOVE ENCOUNTERING INTIMACY WITH HIM AND UNLEASHING HIS PURPOSE FOR YOUR LIFE

I0170477

KEMI OLUTUNBI

SYNCTERFACE™
Syncterface Media
London
www.syncterfacemedia.com

MADE 4 MORE

A DEVOTIONAL JOURNAL

PRESENTED TO

_____

From:

_____

MADE4MORE

21 Days of Experiencing God's Love, Encountering Intimacy With Him
and Unleashing His Purpose for Your Life

ISBN: 978-1-912896-33-2
Copyright © August 2022 Kemi Olutunbi

Cover design by Dami Odukoya Design

Published in the United Kingdom by Syncterface Media, London

To
God the Father,
God the Son, Jesus Christ
and
God the Holy Spirit

Thank You for Your acceptance and love that has defined my life,
altered the trajectory of my life and is taking me
on the greatest adventure of my life.

I am nothing without You,
yet I have everything in You.
I pledge my allegiance to You forever.

Preface

Made4More is a community and tribe of sons and daughters who are passionate about encountering God's love, power, manifest presence and seeing His purposes fulfilled in our generation.

Our desire in all that we do is to experience the love of Father God, intimacy with Jesus and the leading of the Holy Spirit. We believe that we are in our generation to fulfil God's calling, discover and live out our purpose and make a difference in our world.

Our anchor scripture is found in Romans 8:19: *"The entire universe is standing on tiptoe, yearning to see the unveiling of God's glorious sons and daughters". (The Passion Translation)*

We long for an awakening of this truth in our hearts and lives so that God will move in our lives, homes, workplaces, nations and generation. We yearn for our souls and spirits to rise to the truth of this scripture so that we may know the hope of our calling, God's glorious inheritance in us, and His incomparably great power for us.

Made4More is for that someone with a burning passion for Jesus, who longs for more of Him, seeking His heart, not just His hands. It is an invitation from the Father to go deeper into new realms of intimacy with Him. Our life is defined by our mission to know Him and to discover and know ourselves in Him.

Contents

Introduction

God created us for intimacy with Him. One of my favourite scriptures in the Bible is found in 1 John 3:1a

"What marvellous love the Father has extended to us! Just look at it- we're called children of God. That's who we really are". (The Message Version)

"Look with wonder at the depth of the Father's marvellous love that He has lavished on us! He has called us and made us His very own beloved children. (The Passion Translation)

Whenever I read it, I am overwhelmed by God's desire for intimacy with you and me. His love for us knows no end, and He longs for us to draw closer to Him in an intimate and personal way. He longs to reveal His nature and love to you and I as He is a Good Father. His heart for each of us is so large, and it is in knowing Him and drawing close to Him that we find ourselves.

God's original plan for intimacy with us has not changed. In intimacy with Him, we come to realise that we are first sons and daughters, above everything else, and are completely loved by Him. We do not serve Him to be loved by Him; we serve Him because we are loved by Him. Accepting God's love for us in our hearts, not just our heads, is a powerful weapon and tool in God's hands.

You and I are God's glory carriers; we are made for His glory. When God made you, He wove into you unique gifts, talents, passions and attributes for His divine plans and purposes. Your worship to God is not limited to what you do for Him. Far from it, embracing the dreams He has put on your heart and using your gifts and talents is pure worship to Him. When you use your gifts, you are building His Kingdom.

Our highest purpose is to give God glory. When you embrace intimacy with Him and use your gifts, talents, passions, attributes and anointing, you shine and reflect His glory. Our surrender to Him is the beginning and the making of us. As sons and daughters, you and I are called to be a demonstration of the Kingdom of God here on earth. We have been sealed with the Holy Spirit through our union with Christ.

Cultivating and building intimacy with The Father, The Son, and The Holy Spirit is why you were created. it is in intimacy with the Trinity that you find yourself, as you are defined by God's love for you and discover your calling by using your gifts to fulfil His purposes here on earth. Therein lies the key to true fulfilment and pleasing God.

We are not here to find our purpose but to discover it and advance God's kingdom. You are anointed for your purpose here on earth; the anointing of God upon you is His power and presence, His glory which you carry.

Living out your purpose here on earth is important to God and should be important to you. However, when your God-given dreams and desires lie dormant in you, untapped and unrealised, you miss out on experiencing true fulfilment in life as there is a longing in our hearts that can only be filled when we step into our God-given and prepared places.

God has built into you all that you need to fulfil your destiny in Him. This truth should spur you on and colour your daily life. As God's sons and daughters, representing our Father here on earth and fulfilling His purpose for our lives should be our life's vision and mission.

Our greatest pursuit in life ought to be His pursuit; it should define us as each of us has a mission with our name on it, and we can only discover it in God. More than ever, God desires that we be available and willing to serve in His Kingdom. He has the perfect plan for your life and a purpose for you to fulfil in your generation. You are valuable in Christ and understanding this truth is crucial to walking in the fullness of your identity in Christ.

Finding out who we are in Christ, what we have in Christ and what we are living for is the foundation of our Christianity. We are chosen, destined and adopted by God in His love and for His divine purposes. Accepting the treasure in God's word in these simple truths are decisions that determine what paths are laid out for us, what roads are paved for us and the relationships we experience.

You are a designer label. You are created in God's image. You are unique. You have a voice. Your generation needs to hear the message the Father has placed in you. There is no "little me" in the Kingdom because in the Kingdom "little is much". We are reminded of this in 2 Corinthians 4:7:

"We are like common clay jars that carry this glorious treasure within, so that the extraordinary overflow of power will be seen as God's, not ours." *(The Passion Translation)*

"If you only look at us, you might well miss the brightness. We carry this precious Message around in the unadorned clay pots of our ordinary lives." *(The Message Version)*

God is using your life and story (the gifts, talents, passions and experiences) to tell His story. The world is waiting to hear your story, which just happens to be His story too, for His glory. When we don't fully embrace intimacy with God and see ourselves as God sees us, we deny the power of the gospel. Our seats, designed by God, remain unoccupied, and the world suffers.

It is time to take your prepared place. New God-ordained opportunities, ideas and invitations are waiting for you once you say yes to His will. Your place in our Father's heart is secure and does not depend on your performance. My prayer as you use this devotional is that you will encounter God's love for you in a real and tangible way, discover and fully embrace your identity in Christ as a son or daughter and unleash His purpose for your life and your generation.

I pray that the wind of God will usher you into His prepared place for you as you get a deeper revelation of His inheritance in you and propel you into the fullness of your destiny. As you step into the unknown in Him, you will meet with Jesus; you will live out the will and purpose of God in your life and encounter the promise and goodness of God.

May you enter a season of divine appointments (moments in time when you encounter God through His word, people, places and events) that will be significant in God's purpose for your life in Jesus' name.

God is in you. God is with you. God is for you. The world is waiting for you.

In His love and mine,
~ *Kemi Olutunbi*

MADE4MORE
DEVOTIONAL

21 DAYS

OF EXPERIENCING GOD'S LOVE,
ENCOUNTERING INTIMACY WITH HIM
AND UNLEASHING HIS PURPOSE FOR
YOUR LIFE

DAY 1

God's Love for You

(Scripture Meditation: 1 John 3:1a and Psalms 139: 15-18)

Look with wonder at the depth of the Father's marvellous love that he has lavished on us! He has called us and made us his very own beloved children.
~ 1 John 3:1a (The Passion Translation)

When embarking on a journey of deeper intimacy with God, it is important that you know in your head and heart that you are loved unconditionally by God. This can only come through the revelation of the Holy Spirit in your heart. Just like the strength of any building is based on its foundation, so is a revelation of His love vital in your relationship with Him.

A revelation of His love gives you security, value and identity and shapes your choices and day-to-day living. You may have grown accustomed to being loved because of your performance or what you bring to the table and unconsciously bring that mindset into your relationship with Him. But God's love for you is not dependent on your performance.

His love for you only requires you to be yourself, and as you know Him, you will discover who you really are. When you truly accept and receive His love for you in your innermost being, it transforms you from the inside out.

God's love for you is not defined by your circumstances; He loves you. It is a simple truth which has major ramifications when you embrace and begin to live it out. The love of God defines you and affects the trajectory of your life forever.

God's love for you is the foundation of His relationship with you and your walk with Him. You are loved totally and completely.

Heart2Heart
Ask the Holy Spirit to grant you a revelation of God's love for you. Ask Him to show you the areas where you are not living in this truth and the lies of the enemy that you may believe. *(Pray in the Spirit)*

Worship Song
Reckless Love - *Cory Asbury*

Declaration
Father, I thank You for Your love for me. I declare that I am totally loved and accepted by You. I receive my Father's love for me afresh today. I will act out and live out this truth. I am loved and chosen by God. The love of God defines me in Jesus' Name. *(Pray in the Spirit)*

You Are A Living Sacrifice

(Scripture Meditation: Romans 12:1-2 and Psalms 51:1-2)

Beloved friends, what should be our proper response to God's marvellous mercies? I encourage you to surrender yourselves to God to be his sacred, living sacrifices. And live in holiness, experiencing all that delights his heart. For this becomes your genuine expression of worship. Stop imitating the ideals and opinions of the culture around you but be inwardly transformed by the Holy Spirit through a total reformation of how you think. This will empower you to discern God's will as you live a beautiful life, satisfying and perfect in his eyes.

~ *Romans 12:1-2 (The Passion Translation)*

Building intimacy with God requires that we have pure hearts. A pure heart constantly seeks to please Him in all ways. A pure heart is open and honest with God. It is a heart that pours out everything to Him without holding back or pretending, a heart that is naked before God.

It is important that you come before God and ask Him to purge and cleanse you of anything that may not be pleasing to Him; this happens when we are transparent with Him. In the course of our daily living, you and I will miss the mark as God is Holy. But when we come before Him, we need to come with humble hearts, seeking His forgiveness and asking Him to purge us so that the enemy will not have any lien over us by affecting our hearts.

God is a loving and merciful God, yet He is also the judge and Holy one; the blood of Jesus is the penalty that was paid for our sins. The blood gives us access to God as sons and daughters, but we must not take it lightly or treat it carelessly.

To love God is to love what He loves and hate what He hates, and as a living sacrifice, you give up what does not please God, allowing Him to mould and shape you in the way He desires. Your decisions, choices and actions matter to Him. Bringing our hearts before the Lord and asking for His mercy is crucial as the Holy Spirit reveals what is in our hearts, even the things we may not be aware of, which may not be pleasing to God. Our response to God's love for us is to live a life of surrender to Him.

Heart2Heart
Ask the Holy Spirit to search your heart and reveal anything that is unpleasing to God. Ask for forgiveness. Offer your life to Him as a living sacrifice. Ask Him for grace to be willing and obedient to His words. *(Pray in the Spirit)*

Worship Song
Nothing But The Blood - *Travis Greene*

Declaration
Father, I thank You for the sacrifice that You made for me through the blood of Jesus. I declare that I am the righteousness of God in Christ Jesus. I am a living sacrifice, holy and pleasing to God. I do not conform to the patterns of this world, and I am transformed daily by the renewal of my mind through the word of God. My life is pleasing to God, and I walk in His perfect will for my life in Jesus' name. *(Pray in the Spirit)*

God's Unique Plan For You

(Scripture Meditation: Jeremiah 29:11-13 and Ephesians 2:10)

For I know the plans I have for you," declares the Lord, "plans to prosper you and not to harm you, plans to give you hope and a future. Then you will call on me and come and pray to me, and I will listen to you. You will seek me and find me when you seek me with all your heart.

~ Jeremiah 29:11-13 (New International Version)

God has a beautiful plan for your life, which you can only discover in Him. You will only really find yourself when you discover and embrace God's plans and purposes for your life. True fulfilment in your life comes from living out His plans and purposes for your life.

It does not matter how successful you are or what others say about your success if, deep down inside, you know that you are not following the dreams that God has put in your heart. The dreams God put in your heart cry out for expression because God made you to fulfil them. You will not be satisfied until you occupy that place that He has prepared for you.

The starting point is to be submitted to His will, to want what He wants for your life and to accept it. God's best for you is far better than your best dream or desire; I have found that the enemy tricks us into believing that what God has for us is less than what we really desire. God's plans and purposes almost certainly don't always come in the way we desire or expect but ultimately will bring us far more than we could have ever dreamed or imagined.

Our journey with God is made up of lots of different assignments, little ones and big ones, and it all starts with a submitted heart. Letting go and allowing God to fulfil His will through you will amaze and astound you. Yield to His will and say yes to the greatest adventure of your life.

Heart2Heart

Ask the Holy Spirit to grant you a revelation of God's plans and purposes for you. Ask Him to stir up the desires He has for you in your heart. Ask Him to take away every desire that is not in line with His will for you. *(Pray in the Spirit)*

Worship Song

Jesus At The Centre - *Darlene Zschech*

Declaration

Father, thank You for Your plans for my life. I declare that I agree with Your plans for my life and Your desires are my desires. I agree with Your plans to prosper me and not to harm me, and to give me hope and a future. I am God's handiwork created in Christ Jesus to do good works. I will do the good works that God had prepared in advance for me to do. I declare it will be unto me according to God's will and purpose for my life in Jesus' name. *(Pray in the Spirit)*

You Are A Pure Container of Christ

(Scripture Meditation: 2 Timothy 2:20-22 and Psalms 51:10-11)

In a palace you find many kinds of containers and tableware for many different uses. Some are beautifully inlaid with gold or silver, but some are made of wood or earthenware; some of them are used for banquets and special occasions, and some for everyday use. But you, Timothy, must not see your life and ministry this way. Your life and ministry must not be disgraced, for you are to be a pure container of Christ and dedicated to the honourable purposes of your Master, prepared for every good work that he gives you to do. Run as fast as you can from all the ambitions and lusts of youth; and chase after all that is pure. Whatever builds up your faith and deepens your love must become your holy pursuit. And live in peace with all those who worship our Lord Jesus with pure hearts.

~ 2 Timothy 2:20-22 (The Passion Translation)

God created you for intimacy with Him. He longs for you to draw closer to Him in an intimate and personal way so He can reveal His nature to you and live through you. You are God's glory carrier made for His glory. You are called to be a demonstration of the Kingdom of God here on earth and have been sealed with the Holy Spirit through your union with Christ. You carry God's glory, which is His anointing: the power and presence of God.

As we pursue intimacy with God, we need to ask for His grace to walk in His plans and purposes and live consecrated lives for Him. The power of the Holy Spirit on the inside of you empowers you to live a life consecrated to God. First, however, you need to make the decision to do so through your thoughts, words, actions and deeds so that you reflect Jesus wherever you go.

To be a pure container for Jesus is for people to encounter the fragrance of Jesus when they meet you, making God's interest your interest and being sold out to fulfilling God's agenda. Making the knowledge of God your holy and life pursuit, deciding to turn away from the things that are not pleasing to Him and consciously making a daily choice to bring Him glory regardless of what it costs.

To be a pure container for Jesus is to set your gaze upon Him, so His beauty rubs off on you, and you become more like Him so He can live through you as He enables and strengthens you. When we make mistakes, we need to be quick to repent and turn our gaze back on Jesus, knowing we are totally loved and accepted by Him. When we ask God to make us pure containers, souls are saved, and darkness is dispelled.

Jesus keeps us on the straight and narrow path, and the Holy Spirit works in us to do according to God's good will and pleasure as we seek to live with pure hearts before Him.

Heart2Heart

Ask for the Lord to make you a pure container of Christ, dedicated to His honourable purposes and prepared for every good work that He gives you to do. Ask the Holy Spirit to reveal to you what the Lord requires of you. *(Pray in the Spirit)*

Worship Song

New Wine - *Hillsong Worship*

Declaration

Father, thank You that I am a pure container of Christ. I declare that I am useful to the Master and prepared for every good work. I pursue righteousness, faith, love and peace. I dwell in God's presence, and the Holy Spirit leads me on a life of purity in Jesus' name. *(Pray in the Spirit)*

Your Inheritance
~ God's Power In You ~

(Scripture Meditation: Ephesians 3:16-19 and Ephesians 1:19)

And I pray that he would unveil within you the unlimited riches of his glory and favour until supernatural strength floods your innermost being with his divine might and explosive power. Then, by constantly using your faith, the life of Christ will be released deep inside you, and the resting place of his love will become the very source and root of your life. Then you will be empowered to discover what every holy one experiences – the great magnitude] of the astonishing love of Christ in all its dimensions. How deeply intimate and far-reaching is his love! How enduring and inclusive it is! Endless love beyond measurement that transcends our understanding – this extravagant love pours into you until you are filled to overflowing with the fullness of God!

~ Ephesians 3:16-19 (The Passion Translation)

You carry God's power on the inside of you. When we give our lives to Christ, we are granted access to God's power. In fact, you are a carrier of God's power; the same power that raised Jesus Christ from the dead resides on the inside of you. The purpose of that explosive power in you is to fulfil God's plans and purposes here on earth. You are sent by God to bring the kingdom of God into every sphere of influence He has placed you in. You are called by God to use the power on the inside of you to change atmospheres.

The life of Christ is released first in us by His power within us, and then we are called to release it into situations and circumstances around us and in our world. The church – You and I are the world's hope, and as we yield to God, His plans and purposes are accomplished through us. The power of God in us as God's sons and daughters enables us to overcome the enemy's attacks, schemes and wiles so that the Kingdom of God is built through us. We should not be terrified of Satan. Instead, he should be running scared of us because of the great power we carry. The power within you is meant to dispel the darkness around you.

God's love for you, combined with the power within you, is meant to propel you into His prepared places for you to advance His kingdom here on earth. The world suffers when we do not activate the power we carry, as God's plans and purposes cannot be fulfilled through us in our generation.

Heart2Heart
Ask the Holy Spirit to grant you a revelation of the power of God that resides on the inside of you. Ask Him to show you the reason for His power in you and grant you the grace to step out in faith to fulfil His will and purposes for your generation. *(Pray in the Spirit)*

Worship Song
Our God - *Chris Tomlin*

Declaration
Father, thank You that Your power resides on the inside of me. I declare I am strengthened with power through the Holy Spirit in my inner man. I am victorious. Christ dwells in my heart through faith, and I am rooted and established in God's love. I have power through the Holy Spirit to grasp the width, the length, the height and depth of the love of Christ for my fellow Christians and me. I experience the love of Christ, and I am made complete in God's love in Jesus' name. *(Pray in the Spirit)*

DAY **6**

Your Inheritance
~ The Mind Of Christ ~

(Scripture Meditation: 1 Corinthians 2:15-16 and Proverbs 3:5-7)

Those who live in the Spirit are able to carefully evaluate all things, and they are subject to the scrutiny of no one but God. For who has ever intimately known the mind of the Lord Yahweh well enough to become his counsellor? Christ has, and we possess Christ's perceptions.

~ *1 Corinthians 2:15-16 (The Passion Translation)*

You and I, as God's children, have the mind of Christ. What a mind-blowing thought; you have access to divine insights, strategies and revelation. This means if you and I have the mind of Christ, we do not need to grope around in darkness or confusion.

Having the mind of Christ means that we have access to the greatest mind, the one through whom all things that were made were made and will ever be made and the one who is at the beginning and the end at the same time. Therefore, the mind of Christ is crucial to fulfilling His plans and purposes for our lives.

The mind of Christ gives us access to our Father's thoughts; we need not chase after knowledge but rest and embrace what is already ours in Christ. Access to the mind of Christ comes first by acknowledging what we carry and making a quality decision to involve Him in all that we do. Involving Him in the little and big things, asking for His thoughts during our daily living, fellowshipping and cultivating His presence.

Jesus is a good shepherd who wants to instruct and guide us. The mind of Christ is much more valuable than silver or gold. Access to His mind helps us live out His plans and purposes.

Heart2Heart
Ask the Holy Spirit to grant you a revelation of the mind of Christ that resides on the inside of you. Ask Him to forgive you where you have not leaned into this wonderful gift. Pray for God's help to trust in the Lord with all your heart and not lean on your own understanding. *(Pray in the Spirit)*

Worship Song
Lord, I need You - *Passion featuring Chris Tomlin*

Declaration
Father, thank You for the gift of the mind of Christ. I declare that I have the mind of Christ. I have access to revelation, insight and strategies from the throne room of God. I will not be confused or lack knowledge concerning my life's affairs, including God's plans and purposes for me and my generation. I trust in the Lord with all my heart and do not lean on my own understanding. I submit to Him in all my ways, and He will make my path straight in Jesus' name. *(Pray in the Spirit)*

You Are Chosen

(Scripture Meditation: 1 Peter 2:9-10 and Matthew 5:16)

But you are God's chosen treasure-priests who are kings, a spiritual "nation" set apart as God's devoted ones. He called you out of darkness to experience his marvellous light, and now he claims you as his very own. He did this so that you would broadcast his glorious wonders throughout the world. For at one time you were not God's people, but now you are. At one time you knew nothing of God's mercy, because you hadn't received it yet, but now you are drenched with it!

~ 1 Peter 2:9-10 (The Passion Translation)

You have been chosen by Father God. When I checked the meaning of the word chosen, words and phrases such as "Picked out", "Taken in preference", "Elected", "Predestined", "Designated to office", "Selected", "Distinguished" and "One who is the object of choice or of divine favour" stood out. You are God's object of choice, and you are not here by accident. Thinking about God's heart for you should delight you and fill you with joy and peace.

God has called us out, and He gave His most precious gift, His son, Jesus Christ, to die for you and me. We are accepted in the beloved, and we belong to God. God is concerned about every detail of your life. You do not need to live as an orphan, you have been accepted into God's family, and there is a prepared place for you.

You are called to broadcast (relay, spread) His glorious wonders throughout the world. The same mercy we have received we are called to share with others. We are called to share the intimacy we enjoy with Father God, and we share this with others when we make Him known through our gifts, talents, passions, dreams, callings, assignments and anointings. You have been chosen by God to be in this generation at this point in time because you are exactly the person He needs. When others reject us because of our status, background, upbringing, looks etc., we can rejoice and know that we have been chosen by Him.

Being chosen comes with responsibilities. As God's sons and daughters, we each have a responsibility to broadcast His glorious wonders and share His love with others through our stories. God's love cannot be contained; it has to be shared and expressed to others. As kings in the kingdom of God, we bring God's reign and rule into every area. When people encounter us, they have an encounter with the kingdom of God. As priests, we are called to minister to God through our lives as we go about our Father's business.

Everywhere we go is an opportunity and a platform to share God's love, the good news. Make God known through all that you have. It is important for us to take our place in our Father's House and draw closer to Him so that He can reveal His plans and purposes for our lives.

Heart2Heart
Ask the Holy Spirit to grant you a revelation of what it means to be chosen by God. Ask Him to show you your place at His table so you can take your seat and make a difference for His glory in your generation. *(Pray in the Spirit)*

Worship Song
I Know Who I am - *Sinach*

Declaration
Thank You, Father God, that I am chosen by You and set apart for Your purposes. I declare I am a royal priesthood, a holy nation

called out of darkness into Your light. I declare that my light shines before others, and they will see my good deeds and glorify You, my Father in heaven, in Jesus' name. *(Pray in the Spirit)*

DAY **8**

You Are A New Person in Christ

(Scripture Meditation: 2 Corinthians 5:17 and Philippians 2:13)

Now, if anyone is enfolded into Christ, he has become an entirely new creation. All that is related to the old order has vanished. Behold, everything is fresh and new.

~ *2 Corinthians 5:17 (The Passion Translation)*

When you and I give our lives to Christ, an exchange takes place. Before Jesus Christ, we had a life, but now that life is buried as it was in the old nature. Our old lives are gone as we are now made new in Jesus Christ. We are who God says we are.

We receive new spirits, our minds start being renewed as we read and meditate on God's word, and we begin our new life in Christ. Our salvation is a one-time gift that God gives us based on His mercy and goodness.

However, the work of sanctification, i.e. becoming Christ-like, is a lifelong daily process that does not end until we leave the earth. God's work in our lives begins through the Holy Spirit that is living on the inside of us. Your obedience and submission hasten the process, and disobedience and non-submission hinder the process.

The Holy Spirit works in you and me to act in line with God's plans and purposes once we cooperate. Struggles are inevitable in our walk with the Lord. However, God still uses us as imperfect people for His purposes and glory. Whilst our spirits have been made alive in Christ, our bodies are still under the old regime so renewing our minds by the word of God is crucial, as we now carry God's DNA and are made in His image.

With this revelation, you can leave your past life behind and let Him define and give you your new identity. You do not need to hold onto your past life or let your struggle define you. You can leave your past life behind; do not allow past experiences to shape you. Instead, allow your new identity and life in Christ to define you and shape your day-to-day living. Indeed, God makes all things new. You and I are new in Christ; the old life has no power over us.

Heart2Heart
Ask the Holy Spirit to reveal to you what it means to be a new person in Christ. Ask Him to show you how this affects your past experiences and your current and day-to-day living. *(Pray in the Spirit)*

Worship Song
Who You Say I Am - *Hillsong Worship*

Declaration
Thank You, Father God, that I am a new creation, and all that relates to the old order has vanished from my life. I declare that I have been made new in Christ; my past life has no hold on me. I have been set free and made new in Christ. God is working in me, giving me the desire and power to do what is pleasing to Him in Jesus' name. *(Pray in the Spirit)*

DAY **9**

You Have Been Redeemed

(Scripture Meditation: Ephesians 1:7 and Galatians 3:13)

Since we are now joined to Christ, we have been given the treasures of redemption by his blood – the total cancellation of our sins – all because of the cascading riches of his grace.

~ *Ephesians 1:7 (The Passion Translation)*

You and I are the redeemed of the Lord. The word "**redeem**" means *"to gain or regain possession of (something) in exchange for payment"*. We have been bought back from the effects of sins, failures, disappointments and mistakes. The penalty for our sins was paid for by the blood of Jesus.

This redemption releases us from the eternal penalty and the earthly power of sin over us. An exchange took place when Jesus Christ went to the cross and laid down His life for you and me; the resurrection of Jesus changed the course of the world and our lives.

Before the death of Jesus at the cross, we were under the law and had no access to Father God. His death and resurrection purchased our freedom. The freedom and liberty God offers are not the exclusive preserve of certain people. It belongs to everyone!

The benefits of our freedom are not confined to the annals of history. Jesus Christ is alive and crying out for you and I, His bride, to live in the knowledge of this truth. To know that regardless of whatever prison we find ourselves in, the blood of Jesus has paid the price for us and our sins, and we can draw on our covenant rights. Regardless of the devil's accusations, we are free from every form of evil and can live the abundant life that He offers us.

Do not let the enemy steal your inheritance; the blood has availed for every form of sin in your previous life and this new life. We are no longer slaves but sons and daughters with access to God's mercies and riches. We are delivered into love, joy and peace through the Holy Spirit. Your freedom was not free; it cost Him everything. You and I have been endued with all we need to live our lives as God's sons and daughters. The abundant life is available to everyone here on earth.

Heart2Heart
Ask the Holy Spirit to grant you a revelation of your redemption. Ask Him to show you areas of your life where you are living below all that He purchased for you at the cross. Ask Him to forgive you where you have not believed in His promises. Pray for God's help to go after your inheritance and His promises for you. *(Pray in the Spirit)*

Worship Song
Amazing Grace (My Chains Are Gone) - *Chris Tomlin*

Declaration
Thank You, Father God, for my redemption. I declare that I have been bought at a price, and I am free indeed. Free to live the God kind of life. I am joined to Christ, and I have total cancellation of my sins. The past will not hold me back because of cascading riches of God's grace over my life. Christ has redeemed me from the curse of the law. I am a child of God, I have a relationship with my Heavenly Father, and I experience liberty in every area of my life. I am living the abundant life that Christ purchased for me in Jesus' name. *(Pray in the Spirit)*

DAY **10**

You Are Called To Live Fearlessly

(Scripture Meditation: 2 Timothy 1:7 and Isaiah 41:13-14)

For God will never give you the spirit of fear, but the Holy Spirit who gives you mighty power, love, and self-control.

~ *2 Timothy 1:7 (The Passion Translation)*

When you and I give our lives to Christ, we receive deliverance from the spirit of fear which seeks to hold us bound and torment us. You and I are called to live fearless lives without limitations. Fear seeks to hold us and torment us through our thoughts.

Living a fearless life does not mean that you will not be afraid or encounter fearful thoughts, but that you refuse to be held back by these thoughts and press into what God has put on your heart. You refuse to operate from a fear prism or a fear-based paradigm. Instead, you step out, trusting that God who loves you will carry and guide you as your backer, knowing that it is in Him that you live and have your being.

You refuse to be held back by fearful thoughts, but instead, you wage war with the enemy using the word of God, which is the sword of the spirit, against the lies that the enemy seeks to use to hold you captive from fulfilling God's plans and purposes for your life.

We are called to live by faith; we cannot live our best lives without faith. Living a fearless life honours God and helps us fulfil His plans for our lives. We overcome the spirit of fear through the blood of the lamb and the word of our testimonies. When we step out in faith despite how we feel, we are saying, Father God, I believe You, I trust You, You are with me, and You will catch me.

A fearless life is one that lives above limitations with our eyes fully focused on God. When we receive a revelation of God's love for us and accept it, it gives us the security we need to step out in faith and live fearless lives.

Heart2Heart

Ask the Holy Spirit to reveal any area to you where the spirit of fear might be lurking and stealing from your life. Pray for a new level of boldness to come upon you so that you can be all God has called you to be and have all that God has for you. *(Pray in the Spirit)*

Worship Song

No Longer Slaves & Abba - *Jonathan David | Melissa Helser*

Declaration

Thank You, Father God, that you are in me the hope of glory. I have what You say I have, Lord. I can do all things through You, who gives me strength. Thank You for Your gift of boldness and power that resides on the inside of me. I declare that I have soundness of mind and self-control. I am not a slave to fear, and I live fearlessly. I will not fear as the Lord God will help me in Jesus' name. *(Pray in the Spirit)*

DAY 11

Jesus

(Scripture Meditation: Colossians 2:9-10 and John 14:6)

For he is the complete fullness of deity living in human form. And our own completeness is now found in him. We are completely filled with God as Christ's fullness overflows within us. He is the Head of every kingdom and authority in the universe.

~ Colossians 2:9-10 (The Passion Translation)

When we are reconciled to God through our salvation, we also are reconciled to Jesus Christ and the Holy Spirit. Therefore, building our relationship with the Trinity is so important. Our relationship with Father God gives us our identity and security; our relationship with Jesus helps us greatly with understanding and relating with the Father, while our relationship with the Holy Spirit is when it comes to us being guided and knowing the Father's heart.

You and I need a personal revelation of who Jesus is to have a successful Christian walk. Jesus is the embodiment of all that the Father loves. Jesus is also the personification of all that Father God expects from us. He is the Son of God, the firstborn Son and our big brother and Saviour. He is the King in the kingdom of God, and He will reign, and we will reign with Him. He is the Lord of Lords. He is our Bridegroom, and we are His bride; He is constantly speaking His word over us to cleanse and purify us. He is our head, leading us in love, loving us unconditionally and sacrificially. He is the Lion and the Lamb. Jesus points us to the Father, revealing the Father to us; He is the mirror of our Father's love. He is our High Priest, Mediator and Messiah.

There is no Christianity without Christ, everything centres around

Him. We need to think about the Person and the work of Jesus. He accomplished the works of Father God. He existed with the Father from the very beginning, and nothing made was made without Him. He was at your beginning when you were being fashioned. He knows your past, your present and your future. He is the way, truth and life. He is the Prince of peace.

He is the living water that satisfies the deepest longings of our souls. He is the bread of life which feeds us. Jesus is your Saviour, which makes your relationship with Him personal. Becoming like Jesus and knowing Him ought to be the primary pursuit of our lives. Real intimacy with God includes a revelation of who Jesus is.

Heart2Heart

Thank God for Jesus. Praise and exalt Him. Ask the Holy Spirit to reveal Jesus to you. Pray that you will know Him personally and completely. *(Pray in the Spirit)*

Worship Song

What A Beautiful Name – *Hillsong Worship*

Declaration

Thank You, Father God, for Jesus. I declare that I am united with Christ. Jesus is my Saviour. I declare that I will reign and rule with Jesus. I am the bride of Christ. The Prince of peace is mine, and I have peace with God through Jesus. I have access to the Father through Jesus Christ in Jesus' name. *(Pray in the Spirit)*

DAY 12

The Holy Spirit
~ Your Helper ~

(Scripture Meditation: John 14:16-18 and Acts 1:8)

And I will ask the Father, and he will give you another Advocate, who will never leave you. He is the Holy Spirit, who leads into all truth. The world cannot receive him, because it isn't looking for him and doesn't recognize him. But you know him, because he lives with you now and later will be in you. No, I will not abandon you as orphans - I will come to you.

~ John 14:16-18 (New Living Translation)

Our relationship with the Holy Spirit is important as the Holy Spirit reveals Jesus and the Father's heart to us through His leading and guidance.

A personal revelation of the Holy Spirit is crucial to walk in the fullness of God's plans and purposes for you and I. The Holy Spirit is a person. He empowers us to live for Christ. He is our Comforter, Counsellor, Helper, Intercessor, Advocate, Strengthener and Standby.

The Holy Spirit desires a personal relationship with you, and His role in the life of Jesus demonstrates this truth. The Holy Spirit is Jesus's lifelong companion and friend, and the two are never apart. We need to learn to make the Holy Spirit our lifelong companion and friend too. To encounter Jesus is to know the Holy Spirit.

The Holy Spirit makes us aware of God's presence. He reveals the face and the love of God to you and I and unveils the face of the Father so that we might call Him our Heavenly Father, like Jesus, as we have been adopted into God's family. The Holy Spirit makes

His wisdom available to us. He reveals God to us in His Word.

He reveals God to us by giving us His gifts. Without the Holy Spirit, you and I will not have a personal relationship with the Lord. The Holy Spirit comes alongside us to birth God's dreams and desires for us. He helps us overcome challenges and temptations.

To know the Father, Son, and Holy Spirit is to experience true fellowship. We are sealed and marked as God's children with the Holy Spirit. The dwelling of the Holy Spirit within us enables us to experience the fullness of God's plans and purposes for our lives and the presence of Jesus. The Holy Spirit comes alongside us as ministers of God.

The Holy Spirit teaches us all things by illuminating our hearts with truth. He convicts us of sin and leads us to faith. He is holy and teaches us to live consecrated lives to God, transforming us to become more like Christ and helping us in our weaknesses.

The Holy Spirit prepares our hearts so God and Jesus can dwell in us. The Holy Spirit enables you and I to live for the glory of God; without the Holy Spirit, we cannot. He helps us to pray as we ought, praying the perfect will of God in our hearts. Real intimacy with God includes a revelation of who the Holy Spirit is in our lives.

Heart2Heart
Thank God for the Holy Spirit. Praise and exalt Him. Ask the Holy Spirit to reveal Himself to you. Pray that you will know Him personally and completely. *(Pray in the Spirit)*

Worship Song
Holy Spirit, You Are Welcome - *Kim Walker-Smith | Jesus Culture*

Declaration

Thank You, Father God, for the Holy Spirit. I declare that the Holy Spirit guides me into all truth. He lives in and with me. I declare that the Holy Spirit is upon me, and I will be God's witness wherever He sends me in Jesus' name. *(Pray in the Spirit)*

God's Glory

~ His Glorious Inheritance In You ~

(Scripture Meditation: Ephesians 1:16-19 and Romans 8:17-19)

I pray that the Father of glory, the God of our Lord Jesus Christ, would impart to you the riches of the Spirit of wisdom and the Spirit of revelation to know him through your deepening intimacy with him. I pray that the light of God will illuminate the eyes of your imagination, flooding you with light, until you experience the full revelation of the hope of his calling that is, the wealth of God's glorious inheritances that he finds in us, his holy ones!

~ Ephesians 1:16-19 (The Passion Translation)

You and I are designed for intimacy with God. Cultivating and building intimacy with Father God is His desire too. His love for us knows no end, and He longs for you and me to draw closer to Him in an intimate and personal way. He longs to reveal His nature and love to us. It is in knowing Him and drawing close to Him that we find ourselves. There is a famous quote by Jonathan Edwards that says, "The chief purpose of man is to glorify God and enjoy Him forever".

God loves to take pleasure in us, and you and I are His inheritance. He plants dreams, desires, passions and promises in our hearts as His investment in us and longs for us to run with them. You and I are heirs of God and co-heirs with Christ. As God's children, we have an inheritance in Him that can never perish or fade. The Greek word for inheritance used in this verse refers to those who receive their allotted possession by the right of their sonship. We have been adopted into God's family. As God's children, we have full rights to receive His inheritance; we are God's beneficiaries.

This is awe-inspiring! Everything that is Christ is ours. As co-heirs with Christ, we share in Jesus's inheritance. So, what Jesus has we have, what belongs to Jesus also belongs to us. Christ gives us His glory, riches and all things.

As God's glory carriers, it is through intimacy with Him that we possess our glory. Just like Jesus was given glory, we each have a portion of His glory assigned to us. Intimacy with Him leads us to our inheritance. God is our inheritance, and we are His inheritance as He longs for us to fulfil the plans and purposes He created us for. As we know Him, we know who we are. The more we sit at Father God's table and gaze at Jesus's face, the more we know who we really are. Because God is, we are. We are made to carry His glory; we are made for His glory. You and I carry a portion of His glory as He is so large that He cannot be contained in one person. When we take our place as sons and daughters and say yes to His purposes for us, heaven begins to invade the earth through us. You and I are launched like arrows in God's hands.

God uses us like stars in the sky to colour and beautify the world. We colour the world with His light and spread His fragrance. Your worship to God is not limited to what you do for Him. Embracing His truth about you and asking for a revelation of what you carry (His glorious inheritance in you) is a much-needed prayer as there are God-given dreams and desires that are lying dormant in you; untapped and unrealised God visions and desires that are locked up in you which you do not even know about yet. A desire and hunger for your inheritance in Him is pure worship to Him. Our highest purpose is to give God glory. When we get a revelation of His inheritance in us and walk with Him, we shine bright, reflecting His glory and attracting others to Him.

Heart2Heart

Thank God for His desire and longing for intimacy with you. Ask the Holy Spirit to reveal the glorious inheritance of God in you and the hope of your calling to you. Pray for wisdom and revelation that you will know Him intimately and fulfil His dreams and vision for your life. *(Pray in the Spirit)*

Worship Song
So Will I (100 Billion X) - *Amanda Lindsey Cook | Bethel Music*

Declaration
Thank You, Father God, that I have divine wisdom and revelation. I declare that the eyes of my heart are enlightened and that I know the hope of my calling and God's glorious inheritance in me. I will fulfil God's plans and purposes for my generation. God's mighty power is available to me, and I carry God's solution wherever I go. I am His answer to the world in Jesus' name. *(Pray in the Spirit)*

DAY **14**

God Speaks To You, You Hear God's Voice

(Scripture Meditation: John 10:27 and Psalms 32:8)

My own sheep will hear my voice and I know each one, and they will follow me.

~ John 10:27 (The Passion Translation)

God longs to speak to you and me because He cares for us deeply. The Bible is full of stories of God speaking to His people. Hearing God's voice is vital to discovering and fulfilling God's plans and purposes for your life. Without hearing God's voice, knowing His will and fulfilling it is impossible.

Whether you realise it or not, God is speaking to you. Learning to hear His voice and recognising His voice will help you discover God's will for you. It is crucial to staying in His will at all times. The Holy Spirit leads us as we yield to His voice within us. However, it requires us to train ourselves to hear His voice.

When we submit and surrender our hearts to God without preconceived notions of what we want or a personal agenda, we are more able to yield to the voice of the Holy Spirit within us. But unfortunately, our conduct also affects our ability to hear through the Holy Spirit. Therefore, we must honour God through our words, deeds and actions so that the Holy Spirit within us is not grieved.

God wants You and I to involve Him in all our ways. There are many scriptures that tell us how God is interested in every detail of our lives, and He wants You and I to hear Him so that He can lead and guide us, as He is a good shepherd. You heard the voice of God when you gave your life to Him, and the same voice is still speaking to you and will lead you all through your life.

God speaks in different ways, and through different avenues, so we must be open in how we expect Him to talk to us. He speaks through His word and Jesus Christ, nature and creation, God's family, worship music, circumstances, His Holy Spirit, prayer and much more.

You are unique, and God speaks to you in ways that reflect your uniqueness. Hearing God is your covenant right. You are His sheep and the voice of a stranger you will not hear. So, believe He wants to speak to you and that He speaks to you.

Heart2Heart
Thank God for His desire for intimacy with you. Ask the Holy Spirit to lead and guide you in all your ways. Pray for an increase in your awareness of the Holy Spirit and the ability to hear Him. *(Pray in the Spirit)*

Worship Song
All I Once Held Dear (Knowing You) - Prom Praise with All Souls Orchestra ft. Graham Kendrick, Kristyn Getty & Jonathan Veira

Declaration
Thank You, Father God, that You are the God who speaks to me as Your child. I declare that I hear the voice of God, and I will only follow His voice, not the voice of a stranger. The Lord is close to me; He instructs and guides me along the pathway for my life. I will not be stubborn. I will yield to God's promptings and leadings in Jesus' name. *(Pray in the Spirit)*

DAY **15**

You Are Called To Live By Faith

(Scripture Meditation: Hebrews 10:38 and Hebrews 11:6)

And He also says, "My righteous ones will live from my faith. But if fear holds them back, my soul is not content with them!"

~ Hebrews 10:38 (The Passion Translation)

Faith is the currency of the kingdom, and as God's children, we cannot get far without expending it. You and I are expected to our lives by, with and through faith. We have access to God's faith, and as His children, we are not looking for faith out there. The faith we have already exists in God, and we need to draw from Him.

The more we live in God and allow Him to live through us, the more we receive His thoughts and desires. We then exercise our faith in and through Him to fulfil His thoughts and desires that are revealed to us as we are given access to heaven's unlimited resources and power to accomplish His plans here on earth.

We are not the initiators of God's plans and purposes; He is. We need to connect with His plans and purposes so that He can accomplish His desires through us. To have faith is to look at situations and circumstances through God's perspective, not our perspective, which is based on natural situations and circumstances.

There is no other way to live in the kingdom but to trust and obey. Faith is spiritual strength, and the one who has faith will accomplish much for God. Faith leads us to produce good works for our Father.

You and I need to overcome fear as it seeks to hinder the purposes of God for our lives. God is sad and displeased when we do not live by faith as we cannot manifest His inheritance in us. Faith in God causes the timid to become bold. Faith in God causes us to undertake acts of courage and pursue exploits for God's kingdom.

As a carrier of God's glory (honour, wealth, power and manifest presence), your faith should cause every place you are in to encounter a change as heaven is released into the atmosphere. When people come in contact with you and me, they should know they have encountered God in a tangible way through life-changing experiences.

When you gave your life, it was an act of faith. Consequently, to live and fulfil your calling in God will require living a life of faith. Complete reliance on God is what the heroes of the faith are celebrated for; that is what we remember them for.

Faith turns ordinary people into extraordinary people. Faith without works is dead, so it is important to act when we know God's will for us. Even if we are unsure, taking an act of faith is crucial. You and I are designed by God to believe. That is why we are called believers.

Heart2Heart
Thank God for His gift of faith. Ask the Holy Spirit to reveal the measure of faith apportioned to you to fulfil your destiny. Ask God for great faith. *(Pray in the Spirit)*

Worship Song
Oceans (Where Feet May Fail) - *Hillsong United*

Declaration
Thank You, Father God, for Your gift of faith. I declare that I am righteous, and I please You as I live by faith in and through You.

I walk by faith and not by sight, and I call things into this earthly realm from heaven through my faith and obedience to Your word and response to Your love. I exercise my faith and receive all Father God has prepared for me in Jesus' name. *(Pray in the Spirit)*

You Are A Part of God's Family

(Scripture Meditation: Proverbs 27:17 and Ecclesiastes 4:9)

As iron sharpens iron, so one person sharpens another.

~ *Proverbs 27:17 (New International Version)*

As sons and daughters of Father God, we are part of His family and have brothers and sisters that He has chosen. We do not choose our siblings in the Kingdom, He does, and He has designed our destinies such that we cannot do it ourselves; we need our brothers and sisters.

Our brothers and sisters are an intricate part of our destinies. Our life's journey is not a solitary one. Each one of us is a part of God's big plan, and He has put a piece of His plan in each of His children. God has prepared people along our life's path that holds a piece of His plan for our lives, and it is essential that we connect with them. We need to be open to receiving our brothers and sisters as gifts from God created to help fulfil our destiny. There are people on your life's journey that God has positioned in places that you need to connect with to fulfil His destiny for your life. You and I need to be open to God's direction as it may not always be what we think. Remember, one can put to flight a thousand and two, ten thousand.

It is important to ask God to help you recognise and identify the relationships He has prepared for you and build alliances with people who are part of your life's journey. A part of God's vision is in each of us, and as we move on in our life's journey, there are parts of His vision that others carry. We are like parts of a jigsaw puzzle, and we must prayerfully ask the Lord to lead us to our team

(**T**ogether **E**veryone **A**chieves **M**ore) and tribe; those who are sold out to building God's Kingdom and are not after a personal agenda or ambition, those who want God to get the glory in all they do.

God demonstrated a healthy alliance to us through the Trinity; it is the foundation and embodiment of a true partnership. God the Father, the Son, and the Holy Spirit functioning in love and unity. God enjoys seeing healthy interactions and relationships between His children as this reflects His nature. He delights in the diversity within His family and Kingdom. So, we must celebrate and honour God's gift in each member of God's family.

We are called to a covenant relationship with God, and this brings us into His family. When we are invited into God's love, we are invited into communion, relationship and alliance with others in God's family. We are created to be part of God's community.

The right alliances strengthen our convictions and communion with God and propel us into our divine purpose and destiny. Your relationship with God is personal, but it is not private. You and I are called to shine as stars and broadcast God's glorious wonders throughout the world.

Heart2Heart
Thank God for His Kingdom and family. Ask the Holy Spirit to reveal His prepared alliances for you. Pray for God to take you out of every alliance that is not His will for your life. Ask Him to lead and guide you to your tribe and destiny helpers and to prepare people who will help you complete His kingdom agenda. *(Pray in the Spirit)*

Worship Song
Victor's Crown - *Darlene Zschsech*

Declaration

Thank You, Father God, for the gift of family in Your Kingdom. I declare that I build and develop the right relationships and alliances to propel me and others into God's plans and purposes for our lives. I sharpen others, and others sharpen me. Together we have a good return for our labour in the Kingdom. We will bring You glory, Father God, in Jesus' name. *(Pray in the Spirit)*

DAY **17**

You Have A Heavenly Language

(Scripture Meditation: 1 Corinthians 14:2 and Romans 8:26)

When someone speaks in tongues, no one understands a word he says, because he's not speaking to people, but to God - he is speaking intimate mysteries in the Spirit.

~ *1 Corinthians 14:2 (The Passion Translation)*

God has given us a divine and uncommon advantage through the gift of speaking in tongues. The gift of speaking in tongues is your inheritance as a child of God.

Every tribe in the world is recognised by its language, and God, in His love and kindness, designed a language that allows us as His children to communicate in an intimate and unhindered way with Him. It is given to you and me through the empowerment of the Holy Spirit so we can pray in a language only understood by God the Father, Son, and the Holy Spirit. Speaking in tongues is a special and unique language that helps us connect with God's plans and purposes for our lives.

Speaking in tongues is the entrance into the supernatural and miracles; it gives access to the throne room of God. When we speak in tongues, we speak divine mysteries and unlock God's plans and purposes for our lives, hidden treasures given to us as our inheritance in God. Praying in tongues reveals those things that are concealed.

When you and I speak in tongues, we are edified and strengthened on the inside. It builds our trust and faith in God and helps the anointing of God flow through us. It helps us receive the gifts of the Holy Spirit and sharpen our accuracy in God's anointing.

Speaking in tongues helps us hear God and develop a deeper intimacy with the Holy Spirit as we tap into the mind of God. It gives us revelation knowledge and makes the word of God come alive as we read the scriptures.

Praying in tongues helps us develop our prayer life and aligns us to His timing and our God-given assignments. Praying in tongues releases boldness and courage in us. It helps remove limitations as we tap into God's supernatural resources and power and enables us to live a supernatural life. Speaking in tongues helps us produce spiritual fruit.

Speaking in tongues ignites the fire of God in us as we are consumed with a hunger for Him. Praying in tongues is the highest form of agreement with the Holy Spirit praying through us in agreement with Jesus, our High Priest. When we speak in tongues, we praise, worship and thank God. Speaking in tongues helps us conform to the image of Christ. When we pray in tongues, we build and cultivate intimacy with our Father, who loves us so much.

Heart2Heart
Thank God for His gift of speaking in tongues. Ask the Holy Spirit to grant you a revelation of His plans and purposes through speaking in tongues. Pray for His grace to pray in tongues more so you can enjoy all the benefits of your heavenly prayer language. *(Pray in the Spirit)*

Worship Song
The Father's House - *Cory Asbury*

Declaration
Thank You, Father God, for Your gift of speaking in tongues which enables me to speak intimate mysteries to You. I declare that every benefit of speaking in tongues is mine. I declare that through

speaking in tongues, I access my inheritance in God. I align myself with God's perfect will for my life, and I am empowered in my weakness by the Holy Spirit to know how to pray through praying in tongues in Jesus' name. *(Pray in the Spirit)*

DAY **18**

You Have An Inheritance
~ The Scriptures ~
(Scripture Meditation: Matthew 4:4 and Hebrews 4:12)

He answered, The Scriptures say: Bread alone will not satisfy, but true life is found in every word, which constantly goes forth from God's mouth.

~ Matthew 4:4 (The Passion Translation)

The word of God is a treasure in our lives. The Bible is a means of cultivating and building intimacy with God. God gives us His Word to help us know Him. Jesus is the living word; God, His word and Jesus are one. The Bible is the only place where the author reveals Himself, i.e. He shows up as you read about Him. God's ultimate goal is for us to know Him through His word.

As we read, listen and meditate on God's word, our understanding of God increases. The word of God is food for You and I. The more we ingest it, the more it nourishes us and causes us to grow in our inner man and spirit, building up our capacity to trust and have confidence in God.

God's word stored in our hearts gives us light, understanding, and wisdom. It instructs and directs us on how to live our lives. We are called to be both hearers and doers of the word, and we need to allow the word of God to shape and mould us into His likeness.

When you and I believe the word of God, it transforms us and determines the trajectory of our lives. God's word is the ancient path we follow, and as we walk in it, we fulfil His plans and purposes for our lives. The word of God has creative abilities, and listening and speaking the word of God over our lives leads us to endless possibilities in God that we cannot even begin to imagine.

We need to allow the word of God to permeate every area of our life, so we know how to live in the Kingdom. The more you and I spend time in God's word, allowing it to transform our thoughts and actions, the more we are changed and become like God. We begin to think and act like our Father. Our sonship is about resembling our Father; we carry His DNA in us.

We build our inner man through the word of God coming alive in our daily experiences. The word of God always accomplishes the plans and purposes God intends for our lives. Hearing the word of God increases our faith and capacity to receive all that God has for us. You and I need more of God's word in our lives.

Heart2Heart
Thank God for His precious treasure to us in His word. Ask the Holy Spirit to give you a deeper hunger for the word of God in your life. *(Pray in the Spirit)*

Worship Song
More Of You - *Sinach*

Declaration
Thank You, Father God, for Your word. I declare that the word of God will find free reign and rule in my heart. I declare that I will not live by bread alone but by every word that comes from the mouth of God. I will fulfil Your plans and purposes as I receive instruction and guidance through Your word for my life in Jesus' name. *(Pray in the Spirit)*

Transformation & Humility
~ Your Kingdom Mindset ~

(Scripture Meditation: Romans 12:1-2 and Philippians 2:1-4)

Beloved friends, what should be our proper response to God's marvellous mercies? I encourage you to surrender yourselves to God to be his sacred, living sacrifices. And live in holiness, experiencing all that delights his heart. For this becomes your genuine expression of worship. Stop imitating the ideals and opinions of the culture around you but be inwardly transformed by the Holy Spirit through a total reformation of how you think. This will empower you to discern God's will as you live a beautiful life, satisfying and perfect in his eyes.

~ Romans 12:1-2 (The Passion Translation)

You and I are called to live surrendered and consecrated lives in a way that pleases God. We are in this world, but we are not of this world because our mindset is different. We are called to live a life of sacrifice as our lives are not ours but God's. Our lives are devoted and dedicated to His service. Whether at home, work, or wherever we find ourselves, we are obliged to serve Him and live in line with His will in genuine worship.

To live these lives, we need to be malleable to God's will and not given to the ways and whims of the world. We must seek not to live in line with popular culture but be transformed by allowing the Holy Spirit to make us who God wants us to be. When our inner man is strong in the Lord, we can resist the temptations of the world.

We give God both our bodies and mind, allowing His Spirit to transform our minds shaping our thoughts with His thoughts and transforming our hearts. God longs to transform every part of us. Renewing our minds helps us discern God's will as He shapes our thinking and lives.

The Kingdom of God thrives on humility. As sons and daughters of God, we are called to embrace our identity and imitate Christ, our big brother and Saviour. Embracing our identity involves living a life of denial and service to others. Humility is simply recognising and appreciating God's kindness to us and extending it to others, not being arrogant and having the right view of ourselves.

Humility is a sign of godliness; we are called to be humble imitators of Jesus Christ. We trust in the grace of God on our lives and live in a manner that reflects our trust in God. We do not put ourselves forward or try and get ahead at the expense of others. We do not put our own interests above those of others and are not self-centred; instead, we are other-centred.

Being made in the image of God, we are called to reflect the nature and character of God. We express our humility in our submission to God and service to others. To exercise humility is to put our complete faith and trust in God, not relying on the arm of flesh. Humility is a powerful weapon of the Kingdom. In Philippians 2:2-4, we are encouraged to value others above ourselves and not look to our own interests but put the interests of others before ours. Jesus's example in Philippians is one You and I are called to emulate. Humility helps us live in peace and unity with other people. We need to learn to accept correction and not think our opinions and thoughts are always better than those of others.

Humility means we use our gifts and talents for God's purposes, and we do not boast of our accomplishments and abilities. There is nothing that we have that we did not receive from God, and He is the one who accomplishes things through us. God wants to transform and work through us; He longs to use us for His glory.

Heart2Heart
Thank God for His grace that is always made available to us. Ask the Holy Spirit to reveal any area where your mind needs to be renewed and where pride might be lurking in your heart. Ask God for forgiveness. Pray for God to help you live a life that is pleasing to Him. *(Pray in the Spirit)*

Worship Song
Your Love Never Fails - *Chris Quilala | Jesus Culture*

Declaration
Thank You, Father God, for Your mercy. I declare that my body is a living sacrifice, holy and pleasing to God. I do not conform to the pattern of this world, but I am transformed by the renewing of my mind through the word of God. I declare that I will be able to test and approve Your perfect will for my life and live a life of humility which is honouring to You in Jesus' name. *(Pray in the Spirit)*

DAY **20**

You Are Called To Live
The Crucified Life

(Scripture Meditation: Galatians 5:24 and Colossians 3:1-3)

And those who are Christ's have crucified the flesh with its passions and desires.

~ Galatians 5:24 (New King James Version)

You and I are called to live "the crucified life", a life of continual obedience pleasing to the Lord. Our lives are not our own, and the crucified life acknowledges the price that was paid through the blood of Jesus. His death gave us life. Living a crucified life recognises the weightiness of what Christ did for us at the cross and keeping that knowledge at the forefront of our minds and consciousness.

When we give our lives to God, there is an exchange that takes place, where Christ lives through and in us if we submit to His Lordship. We identify with Christ's death and make a heartfelt and conscious decision to live daily for Him in our thoughts, words and deeds. We decide to die to our flesh and yield to Him so we can experience His presence and be pleasing to Him. This shows in our conduct and our character.

We are dead to sin and alive in Christ, meaning you and I are filled with the power of God that makes us dead to sin. Appropriating the power ensures we have victory over sin and life's circumstances. His power also gives us access to the abundant life Jesus purchased for us, including fruitfulness that counts in eternity.

Our will is crucified and subject to His will, and we make daily decisions to live for Him and obey Him in both the small and big things. We seek His will moment by moment. To live the crucified life is to set our hearts on things above, things that have eternal value and things that matter to Him. It means to allow the things that matter to Him to matter to us; to hunger for the things that He is interested in; to live in genuine fellowship with Him; to study and meditate on His word, to obey His commandments; to live a life of stewardship where we offer both our treasure, time and talent to Him. To live a life of love and to love others, to allow Him to fill you and live fully through you. To relinquish control to Him and live a life of faith. To willingly walk away from things, people and places that do not glorify God.

The fire of God burning in you and me is vital for accomplishing God's plans and purposes through us. God uses His fire to expose and eliminate things in our lives that ultimately harm us. His fire helps to keep us burning for Him. The fire of God causes you and I to bring light into darkness. We are called to be passionate lovers of God.

Heart2Heart
Thank God for the sacrifice of Jesus Christ, His Son. Ask the Holy Spirit to empower you to live the crucified life, a life totally submitted to God's will. Pray for His fire to purify you. *(Pray in the Spirit)*

Worship Song
I Will Offer Up My Life - *Matt Redman*

Declaration
Thank You, Father God, that Your grace is available to me. I declare that I have been crucified with Christ. It is no longer I who lives but Christ lives in and through me. I will not be led by my flesh

and its passions and desires. I live my life by faith in Christ Jesus. I set my heart on things above where Christ is sitting at the right hand of God. My life is hidden in Christ Jesus in Jesus' name. *(Pray in the Spirit)*

DAY **21**

Endurance

~ The Key To Obtaining Your Inheritance In God ~
(Scripture Meditation: Hebrews 10:36 and James 1:2-4)

You need to persevere so that when you have done the will of God, you will receive what he has promised.

~ Hebrews 10:36 (New International Version)

You and I will face challenges in our walk with God. As we enjoy His glory, we will also encounter suffering. Trials, tribulations and persecutions are part of our walk with the Lord, but when we face these trials and tribulations, we should consider it pure joy. We should rejoice when our faith is tested because perseverance is produced.

In our walk with the Lord, endurance is needed, so we do not give up before receiving the prize and our inheritance. Patience is a key attribute we need to fulfil God's plans, purposes and promises for our lives. We need to learn to trust God and walk in His timings for our lives, not to run ahead of Him but to wait for His perfect timing so that patience can complete her perfect work in us.

There is always a process of waiting before the manifestation of God's promises. God is working out His purposes in our season of waiting. Waiting well is important to God so that we will be mature and obtain His promise rather than give birth to an Ishmael. An Ishmael is birthed when we take things into our own hands and try to make things happen through our strength and might rather than trust and wait on God to fulfil His promises.

God uses our waiting period to purify our motives as we learn to depend on Him, seek His face and draw strength from His word. Our response during these times is important as it determines if we become better or bitter; a right response makes us better while a wrong response makes us bitter. A wrong response will cause us to miss out on God's plans and purposes for our lives.

It is important to note that trials and sufferings such as persecution, scorn and rejection as a result of our faith are part of our walk with the Lord. However, they are not the same as what the Lord has redeemed us from. Being at the centre of God's will for our lives is the best place to be; it is where we seek to please Him and involve Him in every choice and decision we make, a place where we find His protection and provision.

God uses what seems to be a delay to perfect our faith and teach us to trust Him. Learn to wait well. He is faithful!

Heart2Heart
Thank God for His grace that is always available to you. Ask the Holy Spirit to teach you to wait well and be patient regarding God's promises for you. Pray for God to grant you His peace and help you persevere as you trust Him. *(Pray in the Spirit)*

Worship Song
Gracefully Broken - *Matt Redman ft. Tasha Cobbs Leonard*

Declaration
Thank You, Father God, for the gift of endurance and patience. I declare that I will persevere so that after I have done the will of God, I will receive all that God has promised me. I consider it pure joy when I face trials because I know that the testing of my faith is producing perseverance in me so that I will be mature and complete lacking nothing in Jesus' name. *(Pray in the Spirit)*

MADE4MORE

JOURNAL

21 DAYS

OF EXPERIENCING GOD'S LOVE,
ENCOUNTERING INTIMACY WITH HIM
AND UNLEASHING HIS PURPOSE FOR
YOUR LIFE

DAY 1

God's Love for You

(Scripture Meditation: 1 John 3:1a and Psalms 139: 15-18)

Look with wonder at the depth of the Father's marvellous love that he has lavished on us! He has called us and made us his very own beloved children.

~ 1 John 3:1a (The Passion Translation)

....

....

....

....

....

....

....

....

....

....

....

Heart2Heart

You are loved by God. Ask the Holy Spirit to grant you a revelation of God's love for you. What areas of your life does this truth need to penetrate. *(Pray in the Spirit)*

DAY 2

You Are A Living Sacrifice

(Scripture Meditation: Romans 12:1-2 and Psalms 51:1-2)

Beloved friends, what should be our proper response to God's marvellous mercies? I encourage you to surrender yourselves to God to be his sacred, living sacrifices. And live in holiness, experiencing all that delights his heart. For this becomes your genuine expression of worship. Stop imitating the ideals and opinions of the culture around you but be inwardly transformed by the Holy Spirit through a total reformation of how you think. This will empower you to discern God's will as you live a beautiful life, satisfying and perfect in his eyes.

~ Romans 12:1-2 (The Passion Translation)

....

....

....

....

....

....

....

....

Heart2Heart

You are made for intimacy with God. Intimacy requires holiness. Ask the Holy Spirit to search your heart and reveal anything that is not pleasing to God. Offer your life to Him as a living sacrifice. *(Pray in the Spirit)*

DAY 3

God's Unique Plan For You

(Scripture Meditation: Jeremiah 29:11-13 and Ephesians 2:10)

For I know the plans I have for you," declares the Lord, "plans to prosper you and not to harm you, plans to give you hope and a future. Then you will call on me and come and pray to me, and I will listen to you. You will seek me and find me when you seek me with all your heart.

~ Jeremiah 29:11-13 (New International Version)

....

....

....

....

....

....

....

....

....

....

Heart2Heart

God's plans for your life will bring you the highest fulfilment. Ask the Holy Spirit to grant you a revelation of God's plans and purposes for you. Ask Him to stir up the desires He has for you in your heart.. *(Pray in the Spirit)*

DAY 4

You Are A Pure Container of Christ

(Scripture Meditation: 2 Timothy 2:20-22 and Psalms 51:10-11)

In a palace you find many kinds of containers and tableware for many different uses. Some are beautifully inlaid with gold or silver, but some are made of wood or earthenware; some of them are used for banquets and special occasions, and some for everyday use. But you, Timothy, must not see your life and ministry this way. Your life and ministry must not be disgraced, for you are to be a pure container of Christ and dedicated to the honourable purposes of your Master, prepared for every good work that he gives you to do. Run as fast as you can from all the ambitions and lusts of youth; and chase after all that is pure. Whatever builds up your faith and deepens your love must become your holy pursuit. And live in peace with all those who worship our Lord Jesus with pure hearts.

~ *2 Timothy 2:20-22 (The Passion Translation)*

....

....

....

....

....

....

....

Heart2Heart

You are created to bring glory and honour to God. Ask the Lord to make you a pure container of Christ, dedicated to His honourable purposes and prepared for every good work He gives you to do. *(Pray in the Spirit)*

Your Inheritance
~ God's Power In You ~

(Scripture Meditation: Ephesians 3:16-19 and Ephesians 1:19)

And I pray that he would unveil within you the unlimited riches of his glory and favour until supernatural strength floods your innermost being with his divine might and explosive power. Then, by constantly using your faith, the life of Christ will be released deep inside you, and the resting place of his love will become the very source and root of your life. Then you will be empowered to discover what every holy one experiences – the great magnitude] of the astonishing love of Christ in all its dimensions. How deeply intimate and far-reaching is his love! How enduring and inclusive it is! Endless love beyond measurement that transcends our understanding – this extravagant love pours into you until you are filled to overflowing with the fullness of God!

~ Ephesians 3:16-19 (The Passion Translation)

....

....

....

....

....

....

Heart2Heart

You carry God's power inside of you. Ask the Holy Spirit to grant you a revelation of the power of God that resides inside you. Ask for grace to use the power to fulfil His purposes in your generation. *(Pray in the Spirit)*

DAY **6**

Your Inheritance
~ The Mind Of Christ ~

(Scripture Meditation: 1 Corinthians 2:15-16 and Proverbs 3:5-7)

Those who live in the Spirit are able to carefully evaluate all things, and they are subject to the scrutiny of no one but God. For who has ever intimately known the mind of the Lord Yahweh well enough to become his counsellor? Christ has, and we possess Christ's perceptions.

~ *1 Corinthians 2:15-16 (The Passion Translation)*

....

....

....

....

....

....

....

....

....

Heart2Heart

You have the mind of Christ. Ask the Holy Spirit to grant you a revelation of the mind of Christ that resides inside of you. Ask for God's help to trust Him with all your heart and not lean on your own understanding. *(Pray in the Spirit)*

You Are Chosen

(Scripture Meditation: 1 Peter 2:9-10 and Matthew 5:16)

But you are God's chosen treasure-priests who are kings, a spiritual "nation" set apart as God's devoted ones. He called you out of darkness to experience his marvellous light, and now he claims you as his very own. He did this so that you would broadcast his glorious wonders throughout the world. For at one time you were not God's people, but now you are. At one time you knew nothing of God's mercy, because you hadn't received it yet, but now you are drenched with it!

~ 1 Peter 2:9-10 (The Passion Translation)

....

....

....

....

....

....

....

....

....

Heart2Heart

You are set apart by God and chosen by Him. Ask the Holy Spirit to grant you a revelation of this truth. Ask Him to show you your place at His table so you can take your seat and make a difference in your generation. *(Pray in the Spirit)*

DAY **8**

You Are A New Person in Christ

(Scripture Meditation: 2 Corinthians 5:17 and Philippians 2:13)

Now, if anyone is enfolded into Christ, he has become an entirely new creation. All that is related to the old order has vanished. Behold, everything is fresh and new.

~ *2 Corinthians 5:17 (The Passion Translation)*

....

....

....

....

....

....

....

....

....

....

....

....

Heart2Heart

You are a new creation in Christ. Ask the Holy Spirit to reveal to you what it means to be a new person in Christ. Ask God to help you live this out in your day-to-day living. *(Pray in the Spirit)*

You Have Been Redeemed

(Scripture Meditation: Ephesians 1:7 and Galatians 3:13)

Since we are now joined to Christ, we have been given the treasures of redemption by his blood — the total cancellation of our sins — all because of the cascading riches of his grace.

~ Ephesians 1:7 (The Passion Translation)

....

....

....

....

....

....

....

....

....

....

....

Heart2Heart

You have been bought at a price. Ask the Holy Spirit to grant you a revelation of your redemption. Pray for God's help to go after your inheritance and His promises for you. *(Pray in the Spirit)*

DAY **10**

You Are Called To Live Fearlessly

(Scripture Meditation: 2 Timothy 1:7 and Isaiah 41:13-14)

For God will never give you the spirit of fear, but the Holy Spirit who gives you mighty power, love, and self-control.

~ *2 Timothy 1:7 (The Passion Translation)*

....

....

....

....

....

....

....

....

....

....

....

Heart2Heart

You are created to live a fearless life. Ask the Holy Spirit to reveal any area to you where the spirit of fear might be lurking. Pray for a new level of boldness to come upon you so you can have all God has for you. *(Pray in the Spirit)*

Jesus

(Scripture Meditation: Colossians 2:9-10 and John 14:6)

For he is the complete fullness of deity living in human form. And our own completeness is now found in him. We are completely filled with God as Christ's fullness overflows within us. He is the Head of every kingdom and authority in the universe.

~ Colossians 2:9-10 (The Passion Translation)

....

....

....

....

....

....

....

....

....

....

Heart2Heart

Jesus longs to satisfy the longings of your soul. Ask the Holy Spirit to reveal Jesus to you. Pray that you will know Him personally and completely. *(Pray in the Spirit)*

DAY **12**

The Holy Spirit
~ Your Helper ~
(Scripture Meditation: John 14:16-18 and Acts 1:8)

And I will ask the Father, and he will give you another Advocate, who will never leave you. He is the Holy Spirit, who leads into all truth. The world cannot receive him, because it isn't looking for him and doesn't recognize him. But you know him, because he lives with you now and later will be in you. No, I will not abandon you as orphans - I will come to you.

~ *John 14:16-18 (New Living Translation)*

....

....

....

....

....

....

....

....

Heart2Heart
The Holy Spirit longs for fellowship with you. He is your helper. Ask the Holy Spirit to reveal Himself to you. Pray that you will know Him personally and completely.. *(Pray in the Spirit)*

God's Glory

~ His Glorious Inheritance In You ~

(Scripture Meditation: Ephesians 1:16-19 and Romans 8:17-19)

I pray that the Father of glory, the God of our Lord Jesus Christ, would impart to you the riches of the Spirit of wisdom and the Spirit of revelation to know him through your deepening intimacy with him. I pray that the light of God will illuminate the eyes of your imagination, flooding you with light, until you experience the full revelation of the hope of his calling that is, the wealth of God's glorious inheritances that he finds in us, his holy ones!

~ *Ephesians 1:16-19 (The Passion Translation)*

....

....

....

....

....

....

....

....

Heart2Heart
You are God's inheritance. Ask the Holy Spirit to reveal the glorious inheritance of God in you and the hope of your calling to you. Pray for wisdom and revelation to know Him intimately and fulfil His vision for your life. *(Pray in the Spirit)*

DAY **14**

God Speaks To You, You Hear God's Voice

(Scripture Meditation: John 10:27 and Psalms 32:8)

My own sheep will hear my voice and I know each one, and they will follow me.

~ *John 10:27 (The Passion Translation)*

....

....

....

....

....

....

....

....

....

....

....

Heart2Heart

God longs to speak to you. Ask the Holy Spirit to lead and guide you in all your ways. Pray for an increase in your awareness of the Holy Spirit and the ability to hear Him. *(Pray in the Spirit)*

You Are Called To Live By Faith

(Scripture Meditation: Hebrews 10:38 and Hebrews 11:6)

And He also says, "My righteous ones will live from my faith. But if fear holds them back, my soul is not content with them!"

~ Hebrews 10:38 (The Passion Translation)

....

....

....

....

....

....

....

....

....

....

....

....

Heart2Heart

You are a believer. To have faith is to believe in God. Ask the Holy Spirit to re-veal the measure of faith that is apportioned to you to fulfil your destiny. Ask God for great faith . *(Pray in the Spirit)*

DAY **16**

You Are A Part of God's Family

(Scripture Meditation: Proverbs 27:17 and Ecclesiastes 4:9)

As iron sharpens iron, so one person sharpens another.

~ Proverbs 27:17 (New International Version)

....

....

....

....

....

....

....

....

....

....

....

Heart2Heart

You are a vital part of God's Kingdom and family. Ask the Holy Spirit to reveal His prepared alliances for you. Ask God to lead you to the destiny helpers that will help you fulfil God's kingdom agenda. *(Pray in the Spirit)*

You Have A Heavenly Language

(Scripture Meditation: 1 Corinthians 14:2 and Romans 8:26)

When someone speaks in tongues, no one understands a word he says, because he's not speaking to people, but to God - he is speaking intimate mysteries in the Spirit.

~ 1 Corinthians 14:2 (The Passion Translation)

....

....

....

....

....

....

....

....

....

....

....

Heart2Heart

God longs to build intimacy with you and reveal His heart to you. Ask the Holy Spirit to grant you a revelation of His plans and purposes through speaking in tongues. *(Pray in the Spirit)*

DAY **18**

You Have An Inheritance
~ The Scriptures ~

(Scripture Meditation: Matthew 4:4 and Hebrews 4:12)

He answered, The Scriptures say: Bread alone will not satisfy, but true life is found in every word, which constantly goes forth from God's mouth.

~ *Matthew 4:4 (The Passion Translation)*

....

....

....

....

....

....

....

....

....

....

....

Heart2Heart

God had given us His word as a precious treasure. Ask the Holy Spirit to give you a deeper hunger for the word of God in your life. *(Pray in the Spirit)*

Transformation & Humility
~ Your Kingdom Mindset ~

(Scripture Meditation: Romans 12:1-2 and Philippians 2:1-4)

Beloved friends, what should be our proper response to God's marvellous mercies? I encourage you to surrender yourselves to God to be his sacred, living sacrifices. And live in holiness, experiencing all that delights his heart. For this becomes your genuine expression of worship. Stop imitating the ideals and opinions of the culture around you but be inwardly transformed by the Holy Spirit through a total reformation of how you think. This will empower you to discern God's will as you live a beautiful life, satisfying and perfect in his eyes.

~ Romans 12:1-2 (The Passion Translation)

....

....

....

....

....

....

....

Heart2Heart

You are called to think differently. You have a kingdom culture. Ask the Holy Spirit to reveal any area where your mind needs to be renewed. Pray for God's grace to live out the Kingdom culture..
(Pray in the Spirit)

DAY **20**

You Are Called To Live The Crucified Life

(Scripture Meditation: Galatians 5:24 and Colossians 3:1-3)

And those who are Christ's have crucified the flesh with its passions and desires.

~ *Galatians 5:24 (New King James Version)*

....

....

....

....

....

....

....

....

....

....

Heart2Heart

You are called to live a life of total surrender and submission to Christ. Ask the Holy Spirit to empower you to live the crucified life, a life that is totally submitted to the will of God. Pray for His fire to purify you. *(Pray in the Spirit)*

Endurance

~ The Key To Obtaining Your Inheritance In God ~

(Scripture Meditation: Hebrews 10:36 and James 1:2-4)

You need to persevere so that when you have done the will of God, you will receive what he has promised.

~ Hebrews 10:36 (New International Version)

....

....

....

....

....

....

....

....

....

....

Heart2Heart

You need perseverance and patience to obtain God's promises for your life. Ask the Holy Spirit to teach you to wait well and be patient regarding God's promises. Pray for God to grant you His peace, to help you persevere and exhibit endurance in your walk with Him. *(Pray in the Spirit)*

About the Author

Kemi Olutunbi is a lifelong learner and adventurer who is passionate about people encountering God's love, power and manifest presence and seeing His purposes fulfilled in our generation. She longs for people to discover themselves in God, flourish and excel in their God-given gifts and destinies and fulfil God's calling by making a difference in our world. She believes there is so much more to each of us than is visibly obvious; strengths yet to be discovered, desires yet to be pursued, and dreams yet to be realised. We are made for more.

Kemi is passionate about relationships - marriage, family and friendships - and fulfilling the different roles designed for her by God. However, her most treasured role is as God's daughter, totally and completely defined by His love.

She and her husband, Bode, do life and work together running their businesses and Kingdom expression, "**Lovetalks**". They also run the marriage ministry at their local church in London.

CONNECT

WITH US

AT

www.lovetalks.tv

@LOVETALKSTV

love Talks

DISCOVER FLOURISH EXCEL

www.ingramcontent.com/pod-product-compliance
Lightning Source LLC
Chambersburg PA
CBHW071503070426

42452CB00041B/2279